THE GHOSTWRITER

Mairi MacInnes was born in 1925 in County Durham and educated in Yorkshire and at Somerville College, Oxford. In 1954 she went to live in Berlin and from 1959 to 1987 in America, except for intervals in Mexico and Spain. She has worked as an advertising copywriter, university lecturer, editor, museum secretary, ghostwriter and general stooge. She and her husband live in York. They have four children.

Her first collection of poems was published in Britain and two subsequent collections in the States. In America she won a National Endowment in the Arts Fellowship in 1984 and an Ingram-Merrill Fellowship in 1985, and in Britain prizes in the Arvon, Cardiff and Yorkshire poetry competitions.

She has published two books of poetry with Bloodaxe, *Elsewhere & Back: New & Selected Poems* (1993) and *The Ghostwriter* (1999); and a novel, *The Quondam Wives* (1993) with Louisiana State University Press, which follows an earlier one published in London in the 50s. *The Pebble: Old & New Poems* is forthcoming from the University of Illinois Press.

MAIRI MACINNES

THE GHOSTWRITER

BLOODAXE BOOKS

Copyright © Mairi MacInnes 1999

ISBN: 1 85224 474 7

First published 1999 by
Bloodaxe Books Ltd,
P.O. Box 1SN,
Newcastle upon Tyne NE99 1SN.

Bloodaxe Books Ltd acknowledges
the financial assistance of Northern Arts.

LEGAL NOTICE

All rights reserved. No part of this book may be
reproduced, stored in a retrieval system, or
transmitted in any form, or by any means, electronic,
mechanical, photocopying, recording or otherwise,
without prior written permission from Bloodaxe Books Ltd.

Requests to publish work from this book
must be sent to Bloodaxe Books Ltd.

Mairi MacInnes has asserted her right under
Section 77 of the Copyright, Designs and Patents Act 1988
to be identified as the author of this work.

Cover printing by J. Thomson Colour Printers Ltd, Glasgow.

Printed in Great Britain by
Cromwell Press Ltd, Trowbridge, Wiltshire.

i.m. J.M. and others of Finn's People

Acknowledgements

Acknowledgements are due to the editors of the following publications where some of these poems first appeared: *Columbia, The Hudson Review, The Independent, Lines Review, The New Republic, New Statesman, The New Yorker, The Observer, Poetry Wales, Sewanee Review, The Spectator, Threepenny Review, The Times Literary Supplement* and *The Yale Review.*

An earlier version of the memoir 'Why Poetry?' was published in *The New Yorker.*

Contents

I

11   Travelling North
14   November Digging
16   The Given
17   Hard Lives
18   A Landscape, North Yorkshire
19   Ladies' Lunch
20   The Poppies
21   The Grimshaws
22   In Hospital
24   In the High Woods
25   In the Village
26   Generations
28   Four Kinds of Bird
28   I   *The Dunnock*
29   II *The Dipper*
30   III *The Swallow*
31   IV *The Cock Pheasant*

II

35   The Ghostwriter
38   The Rehearsal
39   Insight
40   Past Histories
40   *The Caul*
42   *Plymouth*
44   *Passion*
46   The Committee Road
48   Finn's People
49   At the Géricault Exhibition
49   I   *The Hussar*
49   II *Carthorses*
50   III *The Kleptomaniac*
52   Missing

54 The Engagement
54 *Prelude*
55 *Prothalamion*
56 *The Fire*
57 *Fact*
58 *Re-make*
59 *The Unravelling*
60 *Con-Man*
61 *Let It Be*
62 *Time and Again*
63 *In the Night*

III

67 Why Poetry?

I

Travelling North

The hills step forward.
I am nearly home

at residue: desperate, derelict;
what lies on its back
in the thick of the wood
between two billows of field;
what hides and sulks, the dud, the fool,
indifferent to rescue.

*

Now it's running for dear life
with its chimneys alive and dead
and mess of roses and the clematis
crawling all over the roof.
What a sight! It is pitiful!
If I catch it I'll give it what for,
and I bet it is filthy,
I bet it can hardly see out,
I bet it is cold and damp,
I bet I'll arrive too late
and it'll just be quiet, big-eyed, shrunk.

*

Here is order, here in passage.
I take a fix on outlying farms'
single brightnesses.
A thousand sheep glimmer along the bank,
all meant, all bargained for.
I storm up in third gear
and look back on a plain
so vast it must contain everything.

Woods, fields, smoke, haze stretch
its pattern to the cathedral towers
and the two power stations'
five cooling towers each,
twenty miles away,
arguments from the silence
under my hissing tyres
repeated again and again as though
I do not take them in.

*

Another ridge, and I plummet down
between high field edges
in ever tighter curves, to a bend
where the odour of muck
sticks, like a sleeping pig,
and there my windows shine
out of their stone and oak
beyond the beech tree and the garden,
beyond the garth, beyond the farmer's
last retaining hedge, beyond this business.

*

It's deathly still in the yard.
Someone is shrinking into the dark
like a fool biting its thumb,
and someone already there,
daemon, or boss, or child
grown tall and critical,
is waiting to put me straight.
The fire will indeed be trim.
Can't I hear the furnace roar?
The beds will be white as brides,
new bread will be hardening,
the sloes disperse in gin
their bluish pungent smoke,
July's hard pickled plums
soften to apricot...

Yes, then, I'm wrong.
Oh, I've been wrong,
oh, far too frequently,
made stupid mistakes, got drunk,
become unmanageable; gone off
without compunction.
What's the difference? – I'm back.

*

The house is waiting, a golden woman.
Her arms are folded, she wears
her contemptuous filial grin.
I'll get out the luggage, go in.
Dear house, I love you best.
Receive me ever kindly as you do now.

November Digging

I am cutting the clearing free from its roots
    Garden will float
free from the adventitious
    the glistening goutweed suckers
ganglias that sprout nettles,
    ivy's furred hawsers
the fibrillations of bramble

Sweet light tents me as I fork
    yet what motes flit
into the corner of my eye and out
    hides and reappears and hides
a small brown knowing bird
    drawn to an exposé of flies
three sharp notes
    but there again he hides

When the black crumb's clear
    I'll plant bushes
gooseberry blackcurrant raspberry
    and one day cheat him of their fruit
punnets of soft
    emerald onyx ruby
for all the pies of summer

But in the interim I fork up
    knobs of clenched bulbs
snowdrop garlic aconite
    and china in blue and white
chipped lustreware and famille rose
    crude pottery with painted bands
a flint sharp as a knife
    a horseshoe oxshoe hinge key bottle
five four-inch nails handmade
    the upper of a boot
who lives down there to need such things

Would he hear if I sang out
    and push up through the soil
his two white hands to clasp my neck
    and show his white face for a kiss
a kiss that would taste of raspberries

The Given

Asthmatic heaven, psychic repletion, air –
the longed-for regimen he long prescribed:
it's here they would have come to spend the day,
in runs and rises where the moors cut loose.
Ecstatic, silent, he'd turn off motor roads
and jolt the Swift down tracks, inch it along
until it stalled. In the end, an ear
to curlews' cries, the whistles grouse invent.
Then, dickey open, he'd get the picnic out.
She'd settle rugs and plates and cups, ignite
the Primus, make the tea. Not what she chose –
lifelong, not what she had in mind. And yet
the warmth of peat and air undid them both.
Below, the old town smoked, the type of hell.

They'd be surprised we too fell in the lap
of hills so casual. Not that we chose
the train to Montreal, the Polish ship,
icebergs off Labrador, the fishing fleets
at ease, the transatlantic haul and thud,
the docks at Tilbury. She'd at least have frowned.
Not what she had in mind. Not what we chose,
either. True, untrue: the toy suburban life
counter and cold. What had it taught us? Flight?
Not what she meant, or he. Things' old shapes
get on with their ancient names, embodiments
of meaning lost, as we ourselves are lost.
The smells of burning wood trash coalesce,
the house of stone comes sailing out of its woods.
A step to the north, moors position themselves;
the skies inaugurate clouds, and winds begin;
the raw ploughed field flickers with rooks and gulls.

Hard Lives

It was foggy and frosty, not a night to be out,
   and there was no one in the village street,
and nothing moved ahead on the lane
   that led between Stocking Farm and larch plantation.
Grass on the verges stared like the fur of some arctic animal;
   the fog came up like a wall at eye-level
and sagged around us like curtains.
   We drove right through it. After all it was easy,
this getting home in winter, we could give lessons

   up to the second when roe deer shot over the headlight tunnel
in the arc of the wipers: left to right funnelled
   leaping grey creatures with delicate wet black
eyes and muzzles – and we cried out in shock,
   that thinned into pleasure because they were free of
the world, and their lives were apart, and their exit as soft
   as bolt after bolt of silk tossed to the floor
of the wood and unravelled. The way ahead was wretchedly bare,
   pot-holed macadam going uphill between fences.

We'd stopped with a jolt. As we re-started, as
   I shifted the gears one by one, as we lost
the fog, climbing, we saw the measure of frost
   stretched over the open field,
the empty barren January field
   (but we'd be home before we questioned anything).
Red eyes in the headlights, shiftings, pale flickerings:
   those were just sheep: solid wool bodies, imbecile faces,
mouths crammed with hay (plenty more hay strewn on the grass).

   It was only days later it hit me how false
perception had been and how misery, what else?
   drew the roe deer from the wood: so famished
they'd fed with the farmer's sheep, so vulnerable they fled
   at the crunch of the car; and more, the world we despised
was open for them to take refuge in
   as it wasn't for us, who weren't secretive, or starving.

A Landscape, North Yorkshire

First there's the map: earthwork and tumulus
   lettered in gothic by the mapmaker;
rivers, farms, woods, hills, lettered in roman
   and named by those who by now are nameless.

The rest is partial, like childhood.
   It's a splinter from the first self
needling under the skin, as something needles
   under these placid pasturing hills.
It's a kestrel soaring up lanes
   so the seam opens between fields,
and hell's beyond, a chasm of mud and water.
   It's the end of a lane in a wood,
at a clearing empty as a pot,
   a sky on it like a blue enamel lid,
on the other side a disused blackthorn tunnel
   with rail ruts a foot deep from traffic
that passed there before macadam,
   and pencillings through winter pasture,
beyond, where the way rounds a contour –
   not the ruled line of the car road,
stiff as a copy, but a curve yielding the weight
   of hoofs and feet and endless thought.

The path photographs that thought:
   let it be sombre, excessive, revolutionary;
reversal in mind, not rescue.
   Recall that a hero went off, promising to write,
and instead came hiatus. Was it death,
   that long silence while it rained and was dark?
He returned long ago. It was spring.
   These fields knew the truth all along,
where he stayed, among these insurgencies,
   these woods with their signs and guns.

Ladies' Lunch

He pocketed one hand and waved the other.
Then I was gone, I suppose, and he went back to that earthy
apartness I fancy he preferred,

and painted, chopped, or scrubbed, and put a record on,
the splendid luminous vacancy of afternoon
fleshed out by the rehearsed emotion

of opera stars whose rival voices
warbled in turn of loves and sadnesses,
regrets, mistakes, and agonies

he might have had to grin at, if I'd been there.
Meanwhile, transfixed in a thunderous hotel bar
I had to read minds like a fortune-teller,

as the bar lacked air and the ceiling pressed down
and bedlam
reigned from the first glass of gin.

I had to touch these other lives, as a child
presses its lips
to the mirror and kisses its very self –

those lizardly eyes, the skin of those cheeks hung loose,
cross-hatched mouths; reticulated necks,
heads bobbing yes, yes;

also their hands' mottle, plus an occasional diamond,
dentists' teeth, laughing; the matched teeth of friends –
a creature forty times sliced end to end

to make tissue sections so neatly successful.
I thought of us wandering the world until
we met at this moment, radiantly whole –

and I saw with relief how we kicked at reunion
as each woman turned, with her own smile of welcome,
and the worm wriggled in me, the sly hermaphrodite worm.

The Poppies

on our sheets came off seed catalogues
on to a three-foot repeat
of 50-50 cotton-polyester, the petals flaming flakes

of Vesuvius, the stamens black, the calyxes
a lurid green and big as babies' heads,
for no-iron designer sleep and sex.

In the shop, on the blind side
of the secret that this was chic,
I'd seen only field poppies and the long rides

we'd take between them. And when the bed
didn't look like a field of poppies
when it was made, but a seed

catalogue, that was a rebuke
for wanting a delineation too clear,
too precise a fulfilment of luck.

The plain white cotton we sleep in now
doesn't speak of a shop.
Like light it says nothing. Its cargo

is light. We sleep as we live,
on blanks like pages still to be written on,
and always between the lines

wildness, the counter-world,
where hunger and its songs crop out
tender as poppies by the high field path
we'll walk on presently, among the stones and drought.

The Grimshaws

We love other people's lives:
we need their focus. Take Grimshaw –
the Mr Grimshaw who killed his wife
and with a hammer,
pursuing her round the table till she fell,
when he put her in the outhouse together
with two of her severed fingers.

No one in the next cottage recognised
so much as a thump.
The postman saw nothing,
nor the man from the gas board
who came to read the meter:
he was turned from the door
with a footling excuse.
Even the travelling hairdresser
thought she must have written down the wrong day.

Nobody at the shop perceived
Mr Grimshaw wasn't the same
as ever, a tidy old incomer,
deaf but polite (the rare times he spoke),
buttoned up in his camelhair coat.
The three mornings after the event
when he picked up his newspaper
were the same as other mornings.

Only the dog frenzied at the window
alerted the policeman to peer in later
and see Mr Grimshaw dead on the sofa
and the blood that spattered the ceiling,
the puddles of blood on the floor,
the wads of human hair.

The postmaster told a reporter:
'They were nice people.' He meant,
the Grimshaws were like us.
When they fell off the shelf and were smashed,
we focused on how we were left,
lopsided and blind, out of money,
instantly recognisable.

In Hospital

I'm an old fool in the guise
of a trusting old fool
and I lie here at one
with a host of other women
somewhere between what we are
and what we think we are

and I think I hear the waves
hurrying inshore one after the other,
fetch of a thousand
thousand waves of generation
and wonder what are the rules
when motherhood's played out
in this world that's a limited whole
and its sides contract
to a women's ward in the hospital

Someone still young
cries in her husband's arms
She came here in the night
I think they've lost their baby,
the woman in her coarse cotton shift
open down the back like a split husk
and the man fully clothed and buttoned and shod
Orpheus who'll return to the light, Eurydice
bound to go under the night with the dead unborn

Better look at the north sky
and the row of terrace houses
on the far side of the railway line
where the Scarborough train slips past hourly,
two silver carriages with a blue stripe
And here is a cheerful monitoring voice
announcing a menu for lunch
(the nurses have been up for hours,
running like flightless birds
in little flat shoes and cockatoo caps)

And now the surgeon appears
in a graceful palais glide
debonair   a little smile   a nice conspiracy
He sits on each bed and explains
he's transferring his power to us
Who knew the future could be so clear?
Now someone is turning us over one by one
with the dispassionate hand of a beachcomber
Someone's going to trim us to the bare root
Oh, why can't I rejoice at being taken up?

In the High Wood

The woods stand clear, glassed in between watcher and watched.
Something's reflected as it moves on the rim of darkness.

Below, a tongue of grass runs in from the field,
and on it a fallow deer flicks its scut and looks back,
moves up to the skyline and looks back again
through the clear glass of the woods, as if all were illusion,
the thought of a solitary, a witness in opposition,
one who did not subscribe to the régime we've grown up in,
who lived at the heart of things once, without fear,
and could never forget it; who decided all at once
he could pretend no more that nothing had happened,
and from then on lived deep and hidden in the clear woods
and waits his chance to change things for ever.

In the Village

Nightfall's at four and the street isn't lit.
We rove hailing each other like fogbound ships.

'Mild for December!' 'Snow for Christmas, though, they say!' 'Aye?'
Overhead's streaked with light, the stars so various
far over moor and field that black shapes in the murk
float away from their moorings of bank and wall and balk,
the nave of the church runs down its slip and floats dangerously near,
nearer than focus allows; but no one will comment
or seek a measurement beyond the old kind signals.

Tomorrow all will be clear. No matter if mistakes are everywhere
and memory is discarded and pressure to read one another
diminished to a sigh. Midwinter nights, relentlessly dramatic
evoke no more than 'How are you?' 'I'm well. And you?'
'This ache of mine's getting no better': shapes throng past
without a true acknowledgement, full of silence, and dispassionate.

Generations

I

Squat, low-roofed, the original
of the great hall attached:
just a farmhouse or a hunting lodge
given slate instead of thatch
made uniform with a coat
of stone and ten-foot windows

tiny grandmother, shtetl-bred,
of well-grown children
who own newspapers and airlines
and television stations and politicians

alone in the dark aware
how lights flood trees and lawn
how car doors slam
how voices expostulate
how thump thump thump
comes up through her feet

she hopes no one will notice her
no one seek her out
till red tail-lights bob off into the dark
to be cut off at the corner
and night fall back as soft
as a shunt of meaning

II

Huge ancestral
    beeches and lindens and oaks
housing whole tribes of birds
    jump and rush through the weather
turbaned and chiffoned in leaves
    loose as the glittering sea

Saplings are tethered to stakes
    enclosed in netting and stiff sleeves
no bird visits them
    they're waiting to grow up
some of them die tethered
    some of them root so deep
the buried earth itself
    considers its part in them
a tunnelling up, a correction of course
    a pair of binoculars.

Four Kinds of Bird

1 *The Dunnock*

As I lay dreaming on the grass
a dunnock flew up to my face,

and fluttered her wings at my eyelashes,
and presented her pip of an eye at my nose

and looked into my pupil
as if she stood on a windowsill

and made of the intervening glass
a mirror of herself, with lawn and bushes,

and the straggling roses and yew hedge,
and the chair under the apple tree, and the ha-ha ditch

rife with rhubarb and brambles.
Or it was the Eden of my skull

she peered into, with a bird
as plain and brown as herself observed

rustling and shifting. My interior
breathed roses and apples. I had her. No escape.
When she took off skywards, the landscape
was bone hard. A petal stuck on the air.

2 *The Dipper*

On the bank of the Wharfe,
   a shock of disbelief –
there, there, under the flowing water
   a bird on the river bed! –
she peered among stones
   and gobbled a grub,
a grub or a water beetle.
   How did she learn to hunt like that,
out of her element,
   holding her breath and
taking the prey by surprise? –
   A small bird with sharp eyes
and untypical behaviour:
   should I regard her as omen,
or gift, or model?

Just as I bent closer
   simply to admire,
she flew into the air
   in a burst of water.

3 *The Swallow*

North of San Diego
    surfer dudes ride the waves
in wetsuits so brilliant
    the colours identify them way out at sea.
Their girls line the beach front,
    swallows on a wire, twittering and balancing,
in days before the winter migration.

The police have a checkpoint two miles north
    for Mexican immigrants without work permits.
Whole families travel for work to Los Angeles
    crammed in the hidden compartments of a truck.
Dogs sniff them out. Sometimes the *sin documentos*
    run across the highway to hide in the desert.
Signs of a fleeing woman and child
    warn drivers to watch out for these figures,
since many have been killed.

4 *The Cock Pheasant*

The reddest of redheads, hung with gold –
ruby earrings, necklace of jet –
cloak of emerald, speckled shirt –
he bursts from the hedge
like a sneeze from the throat.

Mayday, mayday! Universal alert!

The dog alas hangs by a wing.
Oh Louis Seize, he would escape
the dog, the hand, the guillotine!
Oh narrow beak and stiff pink tongue,
an arrowhead stuck in the throat!
Pearlised, oh black spot of an eye!

His corpse afire, I dowse in leaves.
It goes on flaring underneath.
Oh Louis Seize, on my return
I'll take you to a kingly feast!

II

The Ghostwriter

I came to hate the telephone.
I'd leave and make tea and unmissed return

while my subject banged on about love
and her beauty when young – I'd never believe

how she ached when she saw it going!
And there were the husbands and her other men

to be dealt with, and her stage career,
her talent instantly hailed, notices to swoon for,

the command performance in great palaces, et cetera –
Istanbul at her feet, the Middle East, America.

She had our title ready: *Baghdad to Beloit.*
'And so,' I interrupted, 'is that it?'
and heard her sigh 'So..o..o.. Darling, can we meet?'

*

At her elbow I'd sensed the dustiest provinces,
the seediness of Anatolia, the indifference

of Midwestern downtowns; aged Emma Bovary
looking for dues the world would pay

'when our book hits the bestseller list.'
Who said I'd collaborate? I began to protest,

but saw she was braver than I'd admit,
and something rang sweetly in her self-delight.

So I told her sternly she should understand
to write the book I must have a free hand:

the woman must be silent and the image speak.
That image, unlike her, would hold back;

it would be amused, ironic, sensitive,
to tell of a secret self and an inner life

such as her story called for, to give it worth.
'What *inner life*?' she cried, remembering her youth,
when the sole value was herself.

*

In the end she went along, suspicious,
repeating now and then we both were ladies,

as if only a lady would respect her soul,
not lift her life as raw material.

I pointed out the voice was hers,
charged with her marvellous marvellous

charm. Look too, I said, what else I'd given her:
insight, logic, clarity, a biting humour.

At first she felt total joy. And then unease –
obscurely put out, unfocused, travestied.

In six months she exploded: 'This is your book, not mine.
You've made it up. And lots of it is wrong –

not people, or events, or history –
they're fair enough – but me – the heroine isn't me.

I recognise *you* – quite colourless – plain dull:
my life's been rich and gorgeous and beautiful –

I've paid you plenty. What d'you mean, I can edit?
Get it into your little head, it won't fit
me, your sad book. My God, it's quite pathetic.'

*

I returned manuscripts, tapes, transcriptions.
She struggled alone with her own soft fictions

for half a year, couldn't find anyone else
to work for her, and so gave up. Unfinished,

unappreciated, woman and image eyed
each other with distaste over the ink divide.

A pity: she was so elegant, that image! She
would never have owed me money, or thrown my work away.

And nothing left me but wooden spoons, a pair
the woman gave me, carved from one block. I think of her

when I use them in the kitchen every day,
a craftsman's spoons from Konya, in her own country,

with twelve coats of varnish, smooth as porcelain,
the wood clear beneath in colour and grain,
yet harder than wood ever was, as hard as bone.

The Rehearsal

Quiet gathers
   thick as lint
      among the hard chairs.

Summer stands in the street.
   The bare room is
      open and opaque.

The audience crams in
   anonymous, dense,
      then the quartet, slim and quick.

First notes are unclenched,
   They flutter and fan
      and abruptly cut.

A nod, kick start:
   bellies and arms work, piston and crank,
      four crescendos roaring into shallows

climbing a high bank, grabbing or in air,
   stones flying, the quiet
      run through like a village;

and sweating moleskin withers
   and trembling vibrating
      metal handle-bars

and body stepping out of its clothes
   and viewing itelf and quite unafraid
      'I am here,' it says,

'I am here. You have forgotten,
   haven't you? Don't be afraid,
      you will remember now.'

Insight
(to Mairi)

We plunged down from the summit
    over the slither of scree
till the path jack-knifed
    over clints round a baldish moor
and cloughs set in its side
    and welded fields, a hundred of them,
with thorns embedded, and into iron
    woods, faintly aromatic, on a precipice,
harboured in boulders taller than Stonehenge

    till trembling like racehorses
reined back at the starting gate,
    our knees locked, and were agonies,
brakes seized, as stones
    bounded downhill ahead and we stayed,
upright, controlled: we saw
    behind an optic watering screen
the wood, the lake, perfectly black,
    the railway crossing where the train
twice a day gives its excited yelp,
    then the quite invisible house,
roof first (with turrets perhaps),
    and gate ajar, heads swivelling on sticks
from the balconies as we walked in

    wondering what child would dance out then
to meet us – would we know whose,
    the child we had in mind being yet unborn,
her face appearing only in the night,
    her teeth like seed pearls, her eyes
two grains of salt, her hands held out
    for our embrace. Could we refuse
a hesitant child, the one that in fact appeared,
    because we were amazed, fatigued, or shy,
or would we stoop and, heart-stopped, anyway
    gather her into our arms?

Past Histories

The Caul

After a war like that they must have known
nothing was certain — certainly nothing

they privately desired, when simply to wish
more than a life to all meant over-reach,

but still, she being what she was, at Tilbury docks —
February 1919 by memory's acoustic —

on a troop ship from Alexandria,
at full tide drawing to its berth at noonday,

the rails packed with fellows bellowing as one
some ditty like 'My darling Clementine',

she scanned the crowd on the wharf,
face after face upturned, and knew no one
and was unknown,

those on the dock seeing only red faces and O
mouths, hers included, finally joining her parlour contralto

to the single thousand-fold roar. Lost
too her enormous effort, now she was cast away
on the shores of this benighted estuary

far from the waves on Manly Beach and the sun,
and her sisters, and her old sure lover, no one

to meet her. After bitter Greek winters under canvas,
nursing the wounded and malarial, after the deaths and chaos,

wrong-footed. And saw him all at once, full stop:
the hero she had captured, staring up

past her smiles and waves, a stranger
uncouth out of his uniform, whom she felt nothing for.

In the blue light below deck
the unlived years went bad, in the triple bunk,
with shit, vomit, urine, sweat. I think

she'd have wept at such things, and this was worse.
But I am imagining. All I truly know is,

while cranes hoisted kit in great nets
and orderlies toted her trunk ashore, panic

struck her. Then she was met and embraced
and they went off and got married,

and no one knew of the hitch till she told
a niece, on a visit home years later, who spoke of it when old.

Inconsequence. Episode in a long story,
her doubt my diamond, my caul

kept for its luck, seeing she was finally cut
into the pack after all, and dealt.

Plymouth

It could have been worse.
I'd missed my train on purpose

to meet my mother and say goodbye,
believing I mightn't be back for years.

Oh, folly, *folie de grandeur*! The next train ran late,
jammed with troops and dimly lit,

after eight hours entering Plymouth – midnight,
blacked out, bombed out, imaginary port

of embarcation for war. Shouts
of goodbye: the world emptied out;

a hiss and jolt and the slam
of doors and the reek of the spent engine.

So: a night by a gas fire tasting of metal
and the whispering tea-urn of the Salvation Army?

Rather pat with open palms the grid
of gritty brick walls that led

to the shut-fast Y and peal the dim bell.
Two women opened up and gave me hot milk

in the kitchen, while they watched, dependable,
hands in lap, and I drank like a calf from a pail.

My uniform skirt was covered with stains.
They looked and said nothing, for which I was grateful.

In the morning the sun shone,
I went on my way to my Fleet Air Arm Station

believing I'd understood something,
which I hadn't. I arrived as I went on doing,

in an aftermath, when principle
turned awkward, and the air shook with refusal.

Passion

The passion of mourning I entered maturity with
was sullen, erotic, and atheist.

'So he hasn't written? Just as well.'
Without knowing him, my mother could tell.

She liked to play the malign goddess,
whipping up adverse storms and thwarting Zeus,

but a third of the earth was burned,
a third of mankind murdered,

a third of the sea turned to blood –
what did she have to work on, or complain of,

but her glimpse of a single longed for thing
that might not want to be longed for, with my longing

vaster always than explanation.
When the truth came quietly into a crowded room

months later, it couldn't be hailed, or cried out for,
its features being already far too familiar –

and the demobbed man who gave me the news
only looked at me kindly, and was incurious.

I said at home: 'I heard he was killed.'
My mother barely paused. 'Perhaps it's just as well.'

'But only twenty-eight, and after five years of war,
accidently killed? That's not unfair

for a real hero, one of the best,
as everyone said? Don't you think it's a waste?'

That was the fact I thought might
convince her, but fact she would never admit.

So then I left her, unacknowledged,
and in private clung to my rags,

his birdwing smile, and enchanting air of belief
in me – too soon at odds with grief.

The Committee Road

on the isle of North Uist
rushes north and
rushes south

barely used but
by the foreign
MacLeods or MacDonalds
Morrisons or Campbells
who thread it today
bounding in big hired cars
newly rolled off the ferry

Why did they call for a road,
the Committee, why this extra road,
not a race-course for the island ponies

Why not a marina on the Minch
for sailboats and yachts
At the very least, why not,
a monument to the potato
to rival Stonehenge

Because the ponies had been sold off
the women harnessed
to the plough instead
(if there wasn't a little black cow)

Because for weakness
no one could stand to dance

Because the fishing boats
were handled on slips
and the packet from Oban
did nicely without even a pier
Even the emigrant ship
waited out in the bay

Because the potato
belonged to the devil

Because the minister
wouldn't have stood
for any of these things

he who finally took
the Committee Road for the emigrant ship
with most of his people

Finn's People

landed and waited for him
    till the moors darkened
and the seas grew thick.
    After centuries, absentmindedly
and thinking all the while of Finn,
    they took off their old grey heads
and threw them to cap a nearby hill
    so high and deeply nothing could take root.

They trooped then, headless,
    down the path to an unroofed place,
settled their feet in the turf
    side by side in a ring
and addressed themselves to the future.
    By the time Finn came
they'd have turned to stone.
    He must have grieved, unpunctual Finn,
to find a set of slabs
    that once would have got up to bow
and a cairn of heads
    no longer able to weep.

Finn's People, *Pobull Fhinn*, is the name given to a standing stone circle near the cairn of Barpa Langass, North Uist, in the Western Isles of Scotland.

At the Géricault Exhibition

1 *The Hussar*

The stallion rears, his forehooves primed to strike
any assailant who dares approach on foot.
He knows that he behaves as he's been taught.
We think that he is bred to be heroic.
The rider stands in the stirrups, very like
his horse: a beauty, an aristocrat,
perfectly turned out and well equipped, but
not aware as yet he plays with magic.

Crowds bunch and melt before the dazzling paint.
They know it makes them drab, and how for youth
such stylishness and war go hand in hand,
how action magnifies some little truth;
how real death will soon explode a gun
and toss this jewel in the undergrowth.

2 *Carthorses*

Grand and benevolent, but simple like children
roughly reared and fed and taught their trade
and place, that's all, they have their great heads skewed
over their shoulders to see the artist who draws them.
They're on their way to work, one day in London
in 1820, led by their carters, who did
not see either what merited Géricault's lucid
and loving assessment, since they were so common.

Who'd guess that they would vanish from streets
so soon in our time? – the smell of their manure,
the clangour of their hoofs on granite sets,
their skids and snorts, their heaving musculature
vanished, while hussars and their mounts still parade
jingling in procession at the tourist hour.

3 *The Kleptomaniac*

He's clearly mad. It shows in his intensity,
lit from within like a projector that's jammed
and overheating. He sees nothing and
he's not shaken by the painter: or did he,
when all was finished, walk around to see
his features in the paint? And was it a cure
to recognise himself, and to become aware
he was recognised and challenged as a spy?

As for the painter, clearly a man possessed
by the subject's passion, he saw the nothing seen
in the fixed eyes, the horrors of distaste
in the worn mouth. He painted dereliction
as if, near death himself, he found expressed
despair as lunatic as it was human.

Missing

That afternoon, midwinter, yawn
of gloom and damp,
lapsed – collapsed

five and a half hours
into a three-mile walk

and the star
who stepped as light as a dance,
Annie the walker,

shot into the void a self
no bigger than a pellet –

Annie, where
were you, where?
Mother and brother

called into the wind
the sound

of her name, they searched
the night's ditches,
four dark pubs, three dark churches,

two village halls, the better hotel,
the banktop tea-room
shut up after Christmas,

the simple necessary road
empty, no good

to her, oblivious
under the porch light
on the remote ridge farm,

hair dripping under her cap,
clothes wet black,

boots clogged with mysterious mud,
across her face recognition
drifting, alien, diffident, glad.

The Engagement

Prelude

Hundreds of times had I come to that window alone
to take in the woods and fields beyond the gate,
for a charge and reminder. So when we returned

from the iron Western Isles which you hated,
I thought I might lend it to you for a measure
(you had admitted me to your life again).

So we sat on the window-seat looking out
and I gloried as usual. But then you turned your back
and breathed, 'I cannot stand it here.'

A year has gone by. We've just walked in the woods.
I've had no hope of anything,
but the bluebells were out, and you've smiled,

as if a miracle, or else its quiet after-image,
flickered in front of us, and made all true –
the tides of blue and green, the swelling to the sun.

Prothalamion

Hundreds of times have I passed briskly down Stonegate
by the shop where your grandmother's mother
might have naturally halted and strayed

towards its high-waisted dresses and deep skirts
(revelations of ankle and boot): you shot into it
yesterday, shouldering my scruples aside. You bought

a wedding dress in wild silk and a momentous hat –
finest Italian straw and a whirl of tulle.
We wept when we saw you, customers, shop girls and I,

not only because of the price. Great-grandmother's miniature
came sharply to mind. Dead at forty, she left ten daughters
and a confused memory of 'eyes like stars'.

Moreover, I felt sorry, amid the rejoicing,
for the old blue jeans and the brother's shirt
left in the fitting room, with their smell of tobacco and sweat,

and the shattered book on t'ai chi in one pocket
and the way you would always turn contemptuous
from your marvellous eyes in the glass.

The Fire

One time in particular, after night class,
I saw the woods on fire not a mile from home,
a hundred yards in, on the verge of a field,

sheets of flame flapping as though in a gale.
I got out of the car and heard cracking and splintering,
and winced at the yell of light, and felt

heat suckling my hair, and smelled
the nursery hygienics of pine.
There wasn't a soul about.

Home, I tapped in the alarm. Perhaps
they already knew, but the fire-officer,
bright as a star: 'Thanks, we're on our way!'

What happened, I never found out:
screaming sirens, dashing engines, tankers,
hoses, men beating down flames, smoulders, ash?

Or nothing. Impertinence, classed as a false alarm?
The mind jams. This nothing more,
this inability to enquire: it happens to me also

when I think of marriage, mine and others',
imagining what you look forward to,
whether it works, and is happy or unhappy.

Fact

Nevertheless, nevertheless: unmitigated fact –
self-righteous squire – stands in the path
shouting it's his, every damned acre, with no rights of way,

and though I laugh once safe, and know how sceptical
I've every right to be, and let my rambling thoughts make fun
of fact, unmitigated fact, nevertheless, nevertheless,

since once I looked for prehistoric stones,
famous monoliths, supposed to be down a lane,
saw sycamores and telephone poles, scaffolding, some fields,

but not the stones, and sat in the car half-wild,
until the sun came out, and dark fell on the wheel,
and I saw the vast stone overhead,

and there, across the wheat, beheld the next,
and then a third, twenty foot high at least, massive,
and full of mystery: may fact give you such a marriage.

Re-Make

Certain things pain me even now.
Even now, the years tipped out, a rim of salt remains.
Nightly, at three or four o'clock,

a motor-bike trundles through my head
bearing two men, both rigid with laughter
and pain. Daft ercs, they're both drunk.

The rider has extricated from the hospital
the pillion passenger with his leg in a cast,
and they're on their way back to their ship.

The one with his leg stuck out,
his name's still with me. Why remember
this titbit he told me? Where's his whole life?

That lover of yours limps into the room
and I'm appalled. No knowing what may happen
to you. Certain things pain me even now.

The Unravelling

That one time, I thought he was pushing his luck
when I sat in the car at the stoplight and saw you both pass,
him with his limp and you at his side, like

Oedipus blinded by his own hand, my blessed Antigone
his guide. Wrong, though, this man could see,
and no, he felt no remorse, but looped your wrist

with a thong of forefinger and thumb, and, cheek
of the fellow, hitched himself on to your belt,
and rested a hand on your neck.

Why didn't he take one end of a stick
and have you at the other to pull him along
so you'd plod together like one animal?

My life, I thought, had fallen into misuse,
while looking at you both.
I felt hanged by the neck like that hapless

Jocasta, from a lamp, wasn't it, in her own palace?
I turned on the wipers to unfog the view
and jetted some water over the glass.

I can't say the view improved. Where had you gone?
The roads ran out, and citizens appeared
and cut Jocasta down. I put the car in gear.

Con-Man

At the very last moment: 'How dare you!' and so on.
The fabulist advances, with his limp, and his load of years,
and his manly broken smile and clutch of promises –

a diamond and ruby ring, honeymoon in the Maldives,
the Azores, or Caracas, an MG of your own, a Victorian house
by the river, in the bishop's village, a garden at the back,

a vine in a greenhouse, an orchard, a thicket of raspberries.
When you lay on a sunny bank and closed your eyes,
careless of life, 'My treasure!' he exclaimed, and you were all,

all, all his wealth. That boast again! 'Oh, but...' and worse.
He never buys a drink, or pays a bill. He's on relief.
He was never in the Entebbe commando raid,

never crashed in Venezuela, his leg
wasn't hurt in saving passengers and crew,
the girls he 'adopted' were his very own.

The truth comes cranking in. At the very last moment:
'I cannot believe a word.'
This will have been the year we called the police.

If only I'd clobbered the creature and broken his back.
If only we hadn't been glad you were glad.
Again and again we murmur: 'This is ridiculous!'

Let It Be

Everything can wait. People can wait,
and baths, and the wearing of clean clothes
freshly ironed and hung, and the use of the brush and comb.

Display can wait, and the raising of eyelids,
and murmuring, 'Good morning!' 'Good night!'
and 'I am grateful': expensive words now.

And the house, with its armament
of pots and pans, and its ovens and stoves,
its brushes and dusters and buckets of suds:

Let dirt accumulate there, and letters, and the flash
of the answering machine, fax, e-mail, the lot.
Let ash lie in the fireplace, let leaves pile up

in doorways, let windows buzz with flies and dim
with their dottle, let beetles walk with the silverfish
on the kitchen floor, and grubs breed in blankets and gutter.

For you've reached the end of your time. Nothing matters.
At least, nothing matters to you, though the mason nods
through his perspex mask at you as he chips his stone

and the ploughman fast in the tractor cabin lifts
at the headland the enormous eight-fold blades of his plough,
turns, and engages the rig, and mouths at you and grins.

Time and Again

Time and again I'm Demeter, afield on foot
in winter, in search of a daughter, or even her footprint,
or wisp of her skirt stuff in the bare hedge,

a-plod round wood and field, hill and farm, moor and ridge,
with the occasional whistle, or coo-ee, designed not to enrage,
vulnerable as she'd be after Hades' world.

Of course, though, it's winter: therefore she isn't here.
If she were here, it would be spring. A fact simple to remember,
but I forget routinely and drive her wild.

Part of my mind also agrees, in deep hell she is queen
and walks freely and is witty and kind. I see
her radiant among the shades. So much the worse for me,

when I search her out in the bright sun of winter
believing she's lost. Let me be clear about the season –
that, and her summer cry of 'Back off, Mother!'

In the Night

Even as we slept, we became aware of
tearing and munching of grass under our window,
luscious guzzlings and snorts and gasps.
Then came a foldyard cough.

We woke. Three in the morning
and a handful of stars in the very top
of the black, black window.
Annihilation, eyelids down, not terminus.
Dying, shall I hold you by the hand thus?
Pain, is that you? Pain? Pain, is it,

who keeps me alive and out of control?
Who was it said I was too calm,
when all the cheer-up signs were wrong?
Flags, bands, parades, balloons,
even marriage to the queen?

If it was you, you'll be the death of me.
Such moans and wringing of hands!
I mean to be a hundred and one
and always look after you, Pain.

Annihilation is no excuse.
Even with open lids I just can't see.
What though the scene was much the same,
still dark and still Colonus,
the old one and the girl
pretended all was well. At the signal
the old one was carried off,
the girl took up her story,
the famous horses went on eating grass.

III

Why Poetry

'I want you to be dependent,' my mother said. I had been telling her what I wanted to do when I grew up.

Dependent? Forced to stick with her, Mummy's little girl, every secret mocked, exploited, playfully indulged? No, worse, far worse. She meant me to be a fine lady and keep a fine house. The key to this horrible enterprise, it became clear, was marriage to a rich man, whose dependent I would be just as I was hers as a child. He would ensure that I'd never have to do a hand's turn, unlike her, who was not married to a rich man and who, consequently, was busy in the house from morning to night. So my husband would be rich and would dote and I'd be charming.

I wept. I knew I'd never be charming. I didn't want to be charming, I wanted my own way. In any case, we knew no rich people.

'And you shouldn't learn to cook, so your husband will have to provide you with plenty of servants.'

'I shall never marry,' I said.

She stopped laughing. 'You're going to grow up into one of those mannish Highland women like your Aunt Mary.' Aunt Mary was the formidable matron of Glasgow Royal Infirmary. 'Or a B.A.! B.A.s are dirty!'

At the age of nine, permitted to attend school at last, I found several B.A.s, some of them charming women. I discovered other degrees, attached to women doctors, solicitors, dentists, local government officials. They weren't dirty at all. But there was always some grain of truth in my mother's prejudices, and I realised in time that it was the neglected houses of the B.A.s that she objected to, from the unsupervised maids who served tea in greasy china and didn't whiten the doorsteps or polish the brass on the front door, to their families – the husbands with ragged collars and filthy cuffs and stained ties and unpolished shoes, the children with woe-begone faces and pale cheeks and uncertain manners. My mother herself regarded her domestic life as her accomplishment. You could see it the moment you walked over the threshold and saw her tomato-red carpet and her flowers and gleaming silver and old oak furniture she'd carried out of derelict farmhouses and repaired and polished, the pewter plates like moons on the dresser, the brass fenders and scuttles and brass-topped pokers and tongs sunning by the hearth. You'd know it if you ate her good food on good plate, her bread, her cakes, her pies, her spiced beef, her trifle.

So much style was meant to delight and challenge and blackmail. If you like it, love me and copy me, and I will exact your sorrow for the way I slave to create this picture of calm and comfort and pleasure: that was the set of her mind. I turned aside, not permitted to say that the house was boring. I couldn't think how she'd come to the conclusion that it was just the thing for me. Anyway, I didn't see why she was so devious, especially when I compared her schemes with the big above-board deals of my father. If the house pleased her, why was she always complaining, about the maids, the modesty of our income, and her hard work?

Then her campaign medals turned up in a drawer. Medals? Decorations, with their important grosgrain ribbons in moiré reds and blues dangling from a clasp, in a leather box from Spink of Piccadilly, like a soldier's. Fingering them reflectively, my father spoke of life-and-death times when she'd been far from her Australian home, nursing in Greece during the Great War. After such suffering and such labour, life as I knew it should have been pleasant. But she didn't use that heroic and admirable time as a touchstone, she simply put it behind her. She told me it was terrible, and sighed with real grief, and that was it. She wouldn't talk about it. It took me years to discover the truth. She didn't refer to it because she didn't want me to copy her. She said mysteriously that she was ashamed, and I could see that she was being perfectly honest for once. It was hard on her to be ashamed of having been brave, I thought. Yet even in that she was illogical and untrustworthy. 'Your mother is a great snob,' my father said. She thought nice women didn't run off to the war and nurse soldiers. Of course I could not agree, because in this one episode I found her quite wonderful, and whether she was nice or not didn't matter.

Recently an ancient cousin has died, unlocking a hoard of letters, photos and hearsay. Her daughter has also referred me to a book in which photographs of my mother appear, showing her sitting in a kimono outside a bell tent with two other nurses, drinking tea, and picknicking on a grassy hillside with five smiling officers. She carries a white umbrella and wears a hat with a brim and a white dress to the ankles, with little boots showing underneath. The Australian nursing unit to which she is attached has been sent to the 50th British General Hospital at Kalamaria, near Salonika. It is August 1917, two years after the disaster at Gallipoli in which so many Australian soldiers died, and my grandfather has permitted her to leave her private hospital in Sydney and volunteer for service only because he has no sons to send to the war. Nursing is still considered a vulgar occupation, and my privileged mother has had to battle for her training: now at last she is to be vindicated.

The 50th, I have learned through my cousin, was a hut hospital. Other hospitals nearby were in tents. By October 1917 heavy rains caused floods that coursed through the tents and reduced the sites to knee-deep mud. By late November snow fell, driven by gales. The only heating in the wards and the nurses' quarters, mostly under canvas, came from the little traditional charcoal-burning braziers of the Ottoman Empire. Australians didn't know such cold existed. Moreover in August Salonika had suffered a devastating fire which left a huge population of homeless starving people. The docks were so dislocated that medical and food supplies were periodically cut off, and thieves kept raiding the nurses' quarters. There weren't many battle casualties. The beds were full of British and Australian soldiers suffering from dysentery, typhoid, tuberculosis, influenza, and malaria. Many died. My mother too was ill. Her weight sank to under a hundred pounds. Her last bout of malaria happened in a cold London hotel in winter, 1919, when she was quite alone.

And yet – this is the moral, the punchline – she met my father in Salonika. He was a doctor, seconded to the 50th General Hospital from a hospital ship. He was a handsome good man, shy to the end of his days. She liked him, she fancied him, she proposed marriage, and thank goodness he accepted. He told me of her proposal only forty-five years later, when she died. When I laughed with pleasure he was taken aback.

There was only one threat to the idyll, told to the ancient cousin when she was young, and eventually passed on to me. When her ship docked at Tilbury in 1919 after the voyage from Greece, my mother looked down from the deck and saw on the quay the man with whom she was to spend the rest of her life, a man no longer in his beautiful uniform but in a dreadful suit, for whom she felt absolutely nothing. For this creature she was abandoning father, sisters, home and country, a fiancé, friends, and independence? In fact the marriage was a happy one, and my father soon found a better tailor. After that moment of regret she abandoned the past. Even her childhood became short and far away. She officially forgot the number of her sisters as if it were indecent, she forgot her true age, and the method by which my grandfather made his fortune, and of course the Macedonian campaign and the mud and cold in which so many died far from the noise of battle.

* * *

I am pushing a pram to the butcher's, Herr Winkler's, in leafy bourgeois Grunewald in West Berlin. The narrow residential street runs between vast operatic ruins. This is Occupied Berlin nine years after the peace, pre-Wall and post-Air Lift. The boom years are yet to come, but West Berliners observe to each other how fat they are getting.

We cross the footbridge over the tiny Dianasee with its jetties rotting in the water below and its little bandstand for three or four musicians on summer nights in the Kaiser's day. Our dachshund Bloom plunges down a bank and flings himself into the still green water for his daily swim. A citizen stops to inform me that swimming is bad for dachshunds. Their backs, it seems, are frail and can be thrown out of kilter by the paddling motion of huge dachshund paws.

'I know,' I say. *'Leider.'* It seems easier to say so, such is the state of my German. Bloom joins us in a shower of droplets, eager to make a new acquaintance.

'Ach. Ein Dackel der alter Schule!' The citizen beams. There is nothing wrong with Bloom's back after all.

'Swimming seems to make him strong,' I venture.

'He should be on a lead,' says the citizen. 'And where is his official number? You should register him immediately.'

Another citizen has paused helpfully. 'Foreigners do not need to register their dogs.'

'Really?' Both citizens now peer into the pram. More advice follows. The baby kicking and crowing in his nest of blankets and pillows should be wearing bootees. And a hat, a woolly hat. But certainly bootees. A proverb follows. I release a volley of thanks and depart in it.

It twists my soul to feel the object of kindness and at the same time someone belonging to the brutal nation responsible for the ruins and the mountain of rubble cleared from them that was rising in the park. To avoid censure I should follow the incessant advice that perfect strangers feel free to offer me, but I don't because in my mind I feel they should be angry with me, just as I should be angry with them, and the absence of anger on both sides is somehow made tolerable by their unwanted advice and my refusal to heed it. So the dog romps off the lead, the baby goes barefoot and bareheaded. People must recognise without being told that I've crossed into the holy land of matrimony and motherhood and can do no wrong. I am learning to cook, and to be frugal, easy enough, since I've grown up in the war. I study German and attend the remarkable Brecht Theater am Schiffbauerdamm. I write a little poetry and begin another novel. I deal with my husband's terrible depressions, which drag us both to the brink. (How can he be depressed when he is married to me?) Yet we are an anomaly among anomalies, foreigners but German civil servants, exiles while every barracks is crammed with native Germans, refugee Osties from the Russian zone; ex-enemies while a few frail ghosts of prisoners-of-war turn up from camps in Siberia where they have been enslaved for ten years.

The people we know vary from spies and diplomats and soldiers and journalists to the half-Jewish professor who has passed as Aryan and now talks like a freed slave, or the garage mechanic who over a coffee boasts of killing Jews in the Ukraine, or the noble few who have returned from plush exile in America to bring something precious back to the new Germany. They are all unduly representative of something or other, and their differences are earnestly discussed. My husband teaches in the Free University. His colleagues are very old. The students appear middle-aged. One has never seen a cat before. One tells me that in East Germany they wash the linen not once a week but twice a year. They always bring flowers, which they cannot afford, and they do not know when to go home at the end of a party. Their politeness is inhibiting. I long to know them better.

Now I am coming back from the butcher's, the grocer's, the baker's, and the pharmacy, and the pram is full of little parcels. The baby has stopped kicking and lies alert on his pillow looking up at the tree. 'He needs bootees,' says a citizen, stopping to admire. 'A hat too, a woolly hat. You should cover him up. I hope you do not let him play with the dog. Dogs carry disease in their mouths and they lick babies. They are not to be trusted.'

'Thank you,' I say. I wish there was someone to speak my mind to. I would like to tell someone of my son's birth, but no one wants to hear, not even my husband, whose eyes glaze over at the idea of ecstasy. No one is interested. I should write more poems, a sheaf of poems, but who will read them? Those that get published in England bounce off the political situation. I have no faith in what really cries out for celebration. And my mind is wadded with the complacency of pregnancy and childbirth.

It has to be said, in spite of this picture of frustration, that marriage has cut the cackle. The little career has petered out that began with a pamphlet of novice poetry published through John Wain and the great printer William McCance at Reading University.

No more inclusion in anthologies, reduced publication in journals, no more invitations to write reviews, no invitations to read at the old ICA off Piccadilly, no poetry evenings with competent poets at George and Paddy Fraser's in Chelsea; no literary parties where William Empson and Kathleen Raine and Janet Adam Smith are kind to the young; no lunch with Kingsley and Hilly Amis at which they pump me for information about the man I am living with. My novel has been published and Olivia Manning and others have reviewed it generously. But that is that. The baby keeps me at home and prevents me from getting to know German society well enough to use it in a second novel. I do not publish another for forty years. But this is life, I think. My husband has forced me to live.

What is the literary life worth, I ask, missing the bit I knew. Recognition means you write more, for you write to be read, and recognition means readers, and a marketplace to display your wares, and sales if possible, which make possible the creation of more wares. All this subjects the wares to criticism, good and bad. Without such criticism I found myself fumbling in the dark. Similarly, without a familiar and open society to draw from, I was confused, and turned from writing novels to poetry, with its concentrated focus and promise of conclusion. But some recognition would of course have made life easier. It was both inspiring and goading to see my friend Nina Bawden publishing a book a year. I liked her ease and conviction. I liked her vulnerability. I liked what she had to say.

During this immense frustration, it took a long time to appreciate the awkward truths of my new life. On the one side, I was living with someone who understood what I was trying to do and who backed me up. He understood the wish to write because he was a writer himself. He made a space for me in the house and in the time of day. But his effort horrified me, it seemed so untoward and unrewarding. Marriage and motherhood, nevertheless, had speeded things up. No more gazing out of the window. Less hesitancy over the right word.

And yet: Despair. He prized me for the wrong things. Frustration made me sick and violent. There was no leisure and no money to buy leisure. Because my husband was my patron, I felt absurd pressure to write as one of a couple rather than as an individual – especially when it became clear that it was marriage that I should write about. I tried not to write any more. Eventually, though, on a visit, I attended a reading in Edinburgh where I heard three distinguished Scots poets read such rubbish from their work that I knew I could do better, and started to write again. But meanwhile I had crossed the divide, the angry divide between the independent woman and the woman kept at home by her babies. Eyeing my old self across the gulf, I am embarrassed. What is she signalling to me, that self-righteous creature over there? Why is she jumping up and down and shouting? I am looking at her deeply stirred and with my mother's eyes.

* * *

Once or twice my mother has turned up in my poems unbidden. One, called 'I Object, Said the Object', I wrote after moving house from Maine to New Jersey with my husband and our nine-year-old son, and our new baby, six weeks old. In less than a month my husband took off on a mission to Europe. The hall was blocked with packing cases. It was August and hellish hot. The well became poisoned in the drought and started to give dark red smelly water. My milk dried up. Our son, a great comfort, went off to his new school and left me with the baby all day. I was due to go back to my work as a medical editor in a matter of weeks. If I had help in the house I don't remember it. I felt I was drowning and my children were drowning wth me. Just to drive out to buy bread and milk was a major undertaking. I fell asleep in the middle of the day and lay awake at night. Wandering through the unfamiliar garden in moonlight I picked a small fruit like a plum and chipped a front tooth on its stone. Letters from my husband gathered unread. He had gone first to visit my father – my father, not his. It seemed to me that my husband had taken over my life and left nothing for me, not even my father.

This injustice, as I saw it, was too large and imprecise to protest about. And life was unjust anyway, only denying me briefly what it denied other women for a lifetime. Supposing, though, I had complained to my husband before he left and asked him to abandon his mission: he would say, as he'd said before on earlier fellowships and research trips, did I want him to stay home and rot? And I would reply, as earlier, no, if he didn't see the injustice it was already too late. I was not going to argue about justice and demand fair shares. That was beneath me, I thought. I would manage on my own. Other women did. After all, he should be himself. (If I could not be myself, well, it was better and clearer for one person to be himself than for two people, him and me, to be lost.)

Suppose I told my husband that I would not be there when he came back. This is what I should have said, according to two of my friends. But where would I go, with my small entourage? I had no relatives to fall back on, and was not sure that I would have used them anyway. My friends certainly didn't bother to offer me a roof. Even if I took all the money out of the bank and left, it wouldn't last long, and what then? How would I go on with my job without my husband's moral and physical support? The children needed a father. I had made vows. And who was going to make love to me? I couldn't think of anyone else I wished to be in bed with. Suppose I told my husband not to come back: he'd come anyway, bursting open the locks and laughing. I imagined myself to be my husband, faced with a weeping accusing wife, tiresomely flouncing and ridiculous. A poem began itself immediately.

To my surprise, the woman I was depicting as a ravening force of nature, one who angered and wore down the narrator (me as husband) became the Muse, she whom though only an occasional visitor in our house I longed to have as permanent guest. After all, the Muse is only a device. One can switch genders to suit. A woman can play the man quite as well as a man can play the woman. A woman imagines men all the time just as much as a man imagines a Becky Sharp or a Portia or Anna Karenina; her act is not so taken for granted, that is all. The poem ended with the woman calmly addressing the narrator (still me as man), and telling him to bring his sheep, his lambs, the unshorn poems, dear to him but strange, down from the hills of his imagination to a place where they are familiar and fearless. The narrator agrees.

> Heart-full and grateful then I'll bid them come,
>   Their mouths like filmstars' ravaged and remote
>   Uttering sounds unchosen, spontaneous, not
>   Chidden, flocking,
> My lambs, crowding to me, a stranger that says,
> 'What is it that you want? Is it this? Or this?'

As Freud says, What is it women want?

The narrator here (me) turns into the poet, the woman poet as it happens. The lambs are both her children and her poems. I duly sent off this effort to my husband, then in Paris, hoping to wound him and feeling heartsick. A poem was less important than a human being. So the days passed, and the self I'd objectified as the maenad, the wild shouting woman and then the Muse, assumed my mother's face. She was dead by then, and I had no fear of hurting her. She would never have seen herself anyway in what I originally planned as a caricature of myself. There she was, however, in me and also in the Muse, satisfactorily wilful and showing her sharp teeth.

Presently my husband replied from Paris. He had not the slightest idea of the true meaning of the poem and its convoluted history and simply congratulated me on it. Ha, what a thick skin he'd got! Strange, though: on some occasions I had shown him poems only to see him turn red and cry, 'Thanks very much!' as if I'd kicked him. He had simply taken my meaning too personally – a solecism I thought he'd be immune to.

It is very hard to write from the heart of your marriage. Sylvia Plath did it, at terrible cost. Her accomplishment has made the task seem at least possible, though her marriage was unique. Was mine unique? Why didn't I know more about marriage beforehand? Was it worth the effort to write from the heart of marriage, or are we limited to celebration? To write through difficulty made for better poems than to write through ease, not because I despised the gracefulness of ready language, but because sometimes I didn't know what the difficulty really was. I didn't know its shape, its importance generally, or its habitat in language. I thought, rightly or wrongly, that I had to discover such knowledge through the poem itself. For one thing, such difficulty loaded the work with the life – even my life then, trivialised with meeting the needs of my family and household, and haunted by the demands of my job as an editor of medical publications; and paradoxically tormented by the desire to put my own words on paper. The hurt for the poet in me, that mannikin, was marriage, my excellent marriage. The poem I've referred to, 'I Object, Said the Object', represented a first success at getting out of the bog where my feet were stuck. I like to think that things got easier after writing it, but it's taken a lifetime to attach the life to the poetry, and only now that I'm old and have a little leisure and a room of my own, still in my husband's company, do the life and the poetry go along together without falling over every few paces, whipped though they may be by desire.

* * *

But what desire is that, I ask myself today, dissatisfied with these rationalisations. Why do I want to write poetry? Surely not just to work things out, nor to solve riddles, nor for health. To sing, then? To record, to celebrate, to play, to have a good time? For all those reasons. The value of definition varies with the need. Long before art, there was necessity. I understood when my parents were disbelieving ('Did John Wain write that for you?') or scandalised ('Oxford has been the ruination of you!') or bored ('Who is this fellow you keep going on about? He's dead, is he? Probably a good thing.'). The reason for all that nakedness escaped them, as it does me. They sniffed at the eroticism of my verses with horror, as well they might. Why did I go back over my experience, why not leave it alone. It was no better than dog's vomit, that only a dog returns to. In the same manner, a lady asked what I would write about, because I was too young to have anything to say. She meant that I had no conversation. She may not have meant to be personal, but only to imply that she'd seen a lot herself. Also, the silence of others was criticism in itself. Here, a literary life would have come in useful, as when people told me that they knew my husband had done my work, or at least helped me with it, when the whole point was that he was in opposition. They were used to the idea that women did their husbands' work for them – marking papers, acting as their assistants, and so on. Why not, then, let the husband be equally generous; it's nothing for him (they must have thought), he probably ran it off before breakfast.

Disbelief, as I've suggested, stems primarily from the gaze. What was true of parents' gaze was true of a husband's, or children's, or students'. You have only to imagine Rilke writing his *Duino Elegies* on on a campus, his refusal of private ties held against him, his invisible necessity lost, his angels turning away with shielded eyes, to see the advantages of private life in solitude. The private needs of women – poet or plain – tend to be overlooked by the people who are gazing at them. That is particularly striking in the case of Sylvia Plath, whose passion was misinterpreted until Ted Hughes's *Birthday Letters*. And even here some confusion remains over what kind of truth is involved in her poems – the truth of poetry or the truth of who did what to whom.

At least poetry, seen or not, can be practised in private. Perhaps that explains why women are on the whole better writers than painters or musicians. They can work with a pencil on the back of the scrap of paper, like Emily Dickinson or the Brontës, or even memorise beforehand what they will eventually consign to paper, like Irina Ratushinskaya, who was forbidden writing materials in prison. Painters learn their craft in groups, and musicians rely on public performance. Only poets can work stealthily. Not that they always want to, of course; most would prefer what I have now, a good warm room with plenty of light and space to spread books and papers and leave them lying about till a job is over, and the latest in writing machines. And the assumption in ancient Greece that poetry serves a public need and belongs in the public sphere is a delightful one. No question there of being "difficult" and "élitist". Poetry belonged to everyone and everyone appreciated it. Poetry for us doesn't have much meaning until its deeply subjective nature is clear and the authorship of poems attested with photos and little biographies like this one.

And yet – such is poetry's drive towards the impersonal – I once believed poems spoke for themselves. I hated asking for backers. I left unsigned poems on people's tables, something I now see was a girlish thing to do. My husband's assumption that my poems were about him, I have called a solecism, and it shocked me. But I was present and he knew me, and that was his unspoken excuse. Once I read a poem before a university audience about the demands of a house and family and how they came into conflict with my own private work, and I tried to refer to the infinite riches brought by a husband and children which gave rise to staggering contradictions. Afterwards a professor, brushing aside mention of love and riches as so much humbug, asked if marriage were really as bad as all that. Again, a solecism, but recitation of one's own work in public appears to make such a primitive response appear legitimate. There I stood, after all. I'd survived, a perfectly ordinary woman in a nice suit.

So there's this conflict within marriage for a woman poet (it exists for men too, but men appear to be covered by the convention of the romantic poet who isn't a household item in the first place, and who, in the second, glides from one inspiring woman to the next). Writing about the conflict, I put in jeopardy what I have been at great pains to preserve, and for this reason, I suspect: that literature itself is about fidelity and the efforts to escape it, with all the accompanying pains and joys. So have I managed to manoeuvre myself into this difficult position on purpose? And to venture one step further: can it be that writing poetry is not worth it? Look at the amount of bad poetry being written: who can justify that? And yet most good poets have been bad poets once. Can anyone, least of all a woman responsible for children, afford to write badly while mastery is gained, considering the pains and the amount of time poetry demands?

Well, yes. It's easy to come down on the side of the angels, but I think it's worth saying that the effort to write a decent poem and to move people with it is an engagement with the truth, and it shapes your life and, with luck, the lives of others. And more than that: when a poem appears to work, even in my intolerably rough and ready approximations, there's a sublime moment in which all comes together and sheds light.